PLEASE PASS THE SALT...

BETTY BILLIPP

ELIOT HOUSE PRODUCTIONS

Composition and production: Eliot House Productions

Cover illustration: James F. Billipp

ISBN-13: 978-0-61542-785-0
ISBN-10: 0-61542-785-5

All inquiries should be addressed to
Eliot House Productions, 693 Goodwin Rd., Eliot, ME 03903.

Printed in United States of America

12 11 10 09 08 07 10 9 8 7 6 5 4 3 2

Oct. 7, 2015

For Sally –
a new friend I
hope to make an old
friend of.
Betty B.L.

All of the poems in this book have been published previously in the pages of Good Housekeeping, McCalls, The Saturday Evening Post, The Wall Street Journal, *and* Family Weekly *magazine. They are reprinted here with the kind permission of these publications.*

Illustrations are reprinted from original drawings in Family Weekly *magazine, through the courtesy of the artist, Mr. Roy Doty.*

PLEASE PASS THE SALT

"No child of mine," I used to cry,
Before the stork had fluttered by,
"Will ever throw a temper fit,
Or bite or scratch or whine or hit,
Or keep his bottle till he's three,
Or worship cowboys on TV,
Or dawdle so he makes me late,
Or leave his carrots on his plate,
Or act, in short, like other kids
Who make their parents flip their lids.
Heavens no!"
But along with the patter of little feet
Go a couple of million words to eat.

JOINT CHECKING ACCOUNT

My little sins of womankind
(Extravagant, extraneous
Or downright foolish) hide behind
A wily "Miscellaneous."
What crimes, my love, of husbandhood,
Shocking to the female senses,
Are likewise laid to rest for good
Buried under your "Expenses"?

BABY BOOK

Herein we scribed the natal date
Of our first born; his height and weight,
The color of his eyes and hair,
Descriptions of his Teddy Bear.
Ev'ry tooth and curl was hoarded;
For posterity recorded.
Each time he squalled we quoted it,
And when he crawled we noted it.
Our second child? Yes, here's his line:
Born 6 A.M. November nine.

HOW GREEN IS MY VIRUS

Sick, sick, Father is sick.
Call the doc, make it quick.
    Bring him liquids, change the sheet,
    Cool his brow, warm his feet,
    Pull the shades and fetch a pill.
Say you know he's very ill.
    Take his temp, watch his diet.
    Muzzle kids; keep 'em quiet.
    Then when he is strong and perk,
    Send the darling back to work.
Ugh, ugh, Mom's caught the bug.
There she lies, limp as a rug.
    Get an aspirin and a cup;
    She'll feel better when she's up.

NOSTALGIA

I remember a time of life
When I was a child at home,
And boys all carried a pocket-knife
Instead of toting a comb.

FUR SALE

The mink's a buy,
The sable's prize,
But I just try
Them on for sighs.

TEMPER TANTRUM

Faced with this juvenile crisis,
I'm always calm and mature;
As cool as a lemon ice is,
Steady, soft-spoken and sure,
Expression deliberate and mild,
Manner composed and benign;
Provided, of course, that the child
Isn't mine.

GOOD MORNING QUIZ FOR MOTHERS

Who bounded out at dawn again
To get the breakfast on again?
Who wiped up milky spills again
And made them take their pills again?
Who got their noses wiped again?
Whose shoelaces were swiped again?
Who poked in all the nooks again?
And found the missing books again?
Who packed the lunch just-so again?
Who made the ball-point go again?
And when to school they've sped again,
WHO'S GOING BACK TO BED AGAIN?

MY PLOT THICKENS

For inconsistency, regard
The lowly dandelion;
Springs sparsely in my neighbor's yard,
But thickly thrives in mion.

COLLEGE REUNION

In vain you will show them
The snapshots you carry.
For naught you will snow them
With lies about Harry.
Unheeded you'll hint at
Romantic intrigue, dear,
Or boast of your stint at
The Junior League, dear.
For nothing you'll quote all
The places you've gadded;
Just one thing they'll note: all
Those pounds you have added.

P. T. A.

Don't be wise,
Don't be witty;
You'll end up heading
A committee.

ALMOST TOTAL RECALL

I remember where we met;
It was the Joneses' party.
You keep a monkey for a pet.
Your wife is tall and arty.
When you shave, you like to sing,
You think Picasso's tame.
I remember everything,
Except, dear man, your NAME.

GUESS WHO

Her cookie jar is always filled,
He car is at the ready.
She never shouts when milk is spilled,
She lets her kids go steady.
She rings a most indulgent curfew,
Her cooking's like no other.
Who *is* this paragon of virtue?
Why EVERYBODY ELSE'S mother.

TO THE JUNE GRADUATE

His callow, carefree days are through;
Grave problems rule the world he gets—
The first of which is what to do
With seven pen- and-pencil sets!

POLISHING UP FOR THE PROM

The maidens, as nervous as fillies,
All day have been setting their hair;
Washing and pressing their frillies,
Debating which perfume to wear.

They've practiced their smiles in the mirror,
They've tried on their bangles and bows.
And now as the moment draws nearer,
They shine from their heads to their toes.

And what of their escorts, those blooming
Beau Brummels named Tom, Dick or Lars?
They, too, have been washing and grooming—
Their cars.

TO THE WOMAN WHO COMES TO DINNER

If you're blest
With strength to diet,
Be my guest,
But diet quiet!

ACID TEST

Our marriage contract says my guy
Will love me till the day I die;
For better or for worse, forsooth,
In age as well as verdant youth;
In sickness and in robust health,
In times of poverty or wealth;
In taxis or commuter locals,
But will he love me in bifocals?

I LOVE PARIS, BUT . . .

Dior, Balmain and Molyneaux,
I'd like to have a word with you:
I don't care what you do with knees—
Just do it two years running, please!

HOW TO RAISE A BOY

Kiss the hurts and share the joys,
Check his wardrobe, manners, toys.
Straighten posture, teeth and ties,
Teach him never to tell lies.
Shovel in the vitamin,
Fight to make a man of him.
Then someone small named Dawn or Clover
Will dig right in and make him over.

MRS. MACHIAVELLI

I am as wise as twenty owls;
No Solomon has keener been.
So when my children's hi-fi howls,
I simply plug the vacuum in.

I REMEMBER ASPEN

I might have been able to
    cope
With the arms and the legs
    and the knees,
The poles and the gloves and
    the rope,
If I hadn't been wearing the
    skis.

HEARTS AND SHOWERS

Everything was going fine,
Matrimony dandy,
Until this year my Valentine
Sent dietetic candy.

IT'S ELEMENTARY

Historians may seek the reason
For that smile called Mona Lisan,
But I should think that any fool
Could guess: Her kids went back to school.

SPRING FEVER

My love is sprightly as a sparrow,
Full of life and cheer again.
Alas, it isn't Cupid's arrow—
Baseball season's here again.

SATURDAY MATINEE

I am resigned to candy crunching,
To squirming, writhing,
    tickling, punching.
I tolerate the banging seat
As small herds trample on my feet.
Those shrieks and giggles
    do not craze me.
The smell of popcorn fails
    to faze me.
I have not flinched at
    rising price—
But darned if I will see it TWICE!

CROSSWORD-PUZZLE FAN STRIKES BACK

I'm sick of feeling like a dummy;
Tired of thumbing my thesaurus,
Searching for "Egyptian mummy"
Or "an ancient Grecian chorus."
Too often have I come to grief
Via horizontal spaces
For "a Persian bas relief"
Or "olde English garter laces."
This week instead of "long beaked birds"
Or "the female sheep dog's muzzle,"
I'm looking up a few cross words
For that guy who wrote the puzzle.

FIRST GRANDCHILD

Each day our infant orchestration
Begins when dawn is pearly.
I wish the rising generation
Didn't rise so early.

CONSUMER'S REPORT

The pickles, Sir, which bear your label
Are omnipresent on my table.
Their form and color, I attest,
Would rival Grannie's at her best.
All nestled there within the jar,
A perfect masterpiece they are.
In fact, at our house children cry
To taste your pickles. So do I.
So sometime, Sir, perhaps you'll stop off
And show me how to GET THE TOP OFF.

MADAME HOUDINI

Into the washer our socks go in pairs,
And abracadabra, they come out spares.

COMPUTER SUITOR

My digital date's exactly
As advertised for height;
He's handsome and built compactly;
Sports and hobbies are right.
He dances ever so lightly,
And I would be content,
Except he's ever so slightly
Spindled, folded, and bent.

LINES TO A MODEL

I do not like you very well.
The reason why I'm glad to tell:
It's not your smile, your garb, your gait—
But just the fact you wear size eight.

ADVICE TO A MOTHER WHOSE CHILD IS SLOW TO WALK

Ape the worried mother's style,
Pretend the problem's global,
Then beam upon your backward chile
Kids are murder when they're mobile.

AH, THE GREAT OUTDOORS

Ladies, when you've cleaned the fishes,
Pumped the water for the dishes,
Trimmed the lantern, foraged sticks,
Examined sleeping bags for ticks,
And hung your sneakers on the line,
Come over to my tent and sign
My wee petition for stamping out
Camping out.

ARTIFACT

With a vast collection of lotions and cream
My youthful complexion is peaches and scheme.

APRÈS SPREE

With my parka of fox
And my hat loden green,
And my argyle socks,
I'm a sight to be seen.
With my knickers cut short
And big boots a-clopping,
You can guess that my sport
Isn't skiing; it's shopping.

OUR KIDS LOVE BASEBALL

About the bottom of the first,
A frosty drink will slake their thirst.
A little popcorn in the third,
And peanuts in the fifth will gird
Them for the seventh inning stretch;
An interval when Dad can fetch
Them hot dogs, milk, and something sweet
To tide them till it's time to eat.

QUICK, HENRY, MY GARDENING GLOVES

I've roses, iris, larkspur too,
Forget-me-not and poppy;
Incredible in form and hue,
So big they're almost floppy.
You've seen nothing till you've seen
My pansies and my purple phlox.
Ah, yes, my thumb is very green . . .
Leafing through the catalox.

AT LAST—THE SCHOLAR!

Our Junior is boning
Up hard on his book;
No records are moaning,
The phone's off the hook.
And fiercely he furrows
His brow as he quotes
The experts—and burrows
Through pages of notes.
Don't think he is faking
This mad study-fest;
Tomorrow he's taking
His driver's test.

BRACES

We've kept a weekly dental date
For years; it's been a bother,
But now the children's teeth are straight,
And straitened too is Father.

LITTLE MYSTERY OF THE CAR POOL

If Monday Sally's sick in bed,
And ditto MaryJane on Wed.,
And Thursday Peter has the flu,
And Johnny Martin gets it too,
Then how come seven kids revive,
Like MAGIC on the day I drive?

SNOW JOB

Hooray, the world is white with snow,
And though the temp be ten below,
My man will don his winter kit;
Jacket, sweater, scarf and mitt,
Woolen stocking, fur-lined boot,
Plus insulated union suit,
And once bedecked in these, my love'll
Go get the boy next door to shovel.

RITE OF ASSEMBLY

The diagram's explicit:
"Match A and B to bracket,
And if you chance to miss it,
Just check the little packet."
According to instruction,
You "simply snap together
Parts C and D, (the suction
May vary with the weather.)"
The box says "nothing to it;
Join E and F at secant,
So simple kids can do it!"
I hope they can, 'cause we can't.

FOOD MONEY

It goes to pay the garbage man,
The boy who brings the paper;
The fellow in the laundry van,
The sitter when we caper;
The men who manicure the lawn,
Barber kids, or keep 'em shoed.
It goes and goes, and when it's gone,
Mama writes a check for food.

GARDEN PLOT

My neighbors to the left and
right
All garden fiercely, day and
night;
Heroic in their labors.
I watch their produce thrive
and grow,
And disregarding rake and
hoe,
I cultivate my neighbors.

THE CASE OF THE MYSTERIOUS POSTCARDS

While "M"'s in London, "L" and "J"
Inform me they have reached Bombay,
And from Seville a secret pal
Signs "A" for Arthur, Ann or Al.
But, friends, it's hard to care about
Your Technicolor whereabout,
Or on which flight or deck you are,
While wond'ring who the heck you are.

HOPE SPRINGS PATERNAL

As Dad opens the Father's Day socks and ties,
A faraway look appears in his eyes;
He harbors a hope both wistful and rash:
Maybe this year they all paid cash.

HOME FOR THE HOLIDAY

When Junior comes from college,
All his bags cost extra fare.
I guess it's common knowledge
Kids need lots of stuff to wear.
Yet with 80 pounds of gear,
Our youthful fashion expert
Every morning will appear
In the same blue jeans and sweat shirt.

DEAR MR. POSTMASTER

While First Class is quivery,
And Second may fail,
Neither winds that are shivery
Nor ice, sleet, or hail
Will halt the delivery
Of "Occupant" mail.

'TWAS THE NIGHT BEFORE VALENTINE'S

Stores have all closed, and alack,
High tragedy's come to pass:
Twenty-four cards in the pack;
Twenty-five kids in the class.

INSTANT FACTS OF LIFE

Time was when Papa painfully
Told fables of the bird and bee
And hemmed and hawed and filled the void
With quotes from Darwin and from Freud.
But that was in the long ago,
When sons and fathers both were slow.
These days it's simpler; modern dads
Just let 'em read the movie ads.

FATHER CLEANS THE BASEMENT

Ah, at last my love is sweeping
Out the treasures he's been saving;
Rusty relics he's been keeping,
Notwithstanding all my raving.
Ribbons, trophies, books, and letters
From his high-school graduation,
Ancient hats and shoes and sweaters;
Twenty years' accumulation.
Can it be he's going to ditch 'em?
My delight would be ecstatic!
Silly girl! He plans to switch 'em
From the cellar to the attic.

THE JOKER'S ON US

Playing cards? We've pecks of them,
At least a dozen decks of them—
Red and green and blue and peach—
Exactly 51 of each.

MAN AND SUPERMARKET

Three brown bags are packed
With the items that he spent for;
Everything, in fact,
But the item he was sent for.

V FOR VACATION

Mind your P's, mind your Q's,
Mind your philodendrons, too.
Mind your poodles, mind your pets,
Find them lodging at the vet's.
Mind ALL your flora and your fauna,
'Cause this year, neighbors, I'm not gonna.

SADISTIC STATISTIC

The kindergarten teacher's sweet,
But when it rains she blubbers,
'Cause thirty pairs of little feet
Add up to sixty rubbers.

MOM WATCHES TV FOOTBALL

I'm alert and full of verve
As I check the coach's call.
My attention does not swerve
From big Number Nine at all.
I can see him cut and curve,
See him tackled, see him fall;
And it's *then* that I observe
Number Twenty had the ball.

FOND PARENTS
AT GRADUATION EXERCISES

You see the child who's speaking now?
The one who made the graceful bow?
Her poise is something to behold;
Her knees are steady, gestures bold,
Her diction's perfect, posture's fine,
She hasn't missed a single line,
And really I'd enjoy her text—
If only Junior weren't on next!

MUCH ADIEU

The cock is crowing;
I stifle a yawn.
They're going, going,
But never gone.

DIARY OF A DEJECTED DIETER

I've taken every fad up,
But lately I've a sinking
Feeling they don't add up
To more than wishful shrinking.

LAST RESORT WEAR

That couturier genius
Who wants to Bikini us
Will first have to teeny us
Betwixt and betweenious.

LADY CAMPERS, RELAX!

That rustling hiss which sounds like bear
On your first night sleeping out
Is not a bear; it's just the air
In your mattress seeping out.

GOOD HUMOR MAN

My husband is mellow,
The mildest of men;
A sweet-tempered fellow
Who's smoking again.

TRAVELER'S CHECK

With suitcase packed, my maps unfurled,
And vaccination aflame,
I felt a woman of the world,
Till my passport picture came.

HIGH NOON

Let's be merry, let's be mad,
Let's be crazy and not curb it.
Let's be daring, let's be bad;
Let's order pie instead of sherbet.

LAWN BOY

Father lines up all the dates,
Checks the mowers and the rates.
Sister answers shrilling phones,
Adjusts the schedule, hears
    the groans
Of customers. Mom corners son
And hounds him till the task
    is done.
Then Junior, pocketing the pelf,
Says, "Gee! I earned it all myself!"

THE EYES HAVE IT

This morning I hid
In my bath to apply
Pale purple to lid
And old gold under eye.
I deepened the tint
Of my brows with a splash,
And tossed on a hint
Of burnt bronze to each lash.
I followed the book,
Though it took me till noon,
And how do I look?
Like a sexy raccoon.

WHEN THE SAINTS GO MARCHING IN

Those early martyrs strong and steady
Did deeds that would unnerve us.
But did they get four children ready
For the nine-thirty service?

HAPPY ANNIVERSARY

Chill the wine and light the tapers,
Fetch his slippers and the papers,
Fill the silver bowl with flowers,
Play that record known as "ours,"
Then brace yourself—he's going to say:
"Have we got something on today?"

WAITRESS WATCHING

Oh, how I wish, just once, that she
From kitchen regions nether,
Would bring my sandwich and my tea
Together.

TAKE ME OUT TO THE BALL GAME

Hooray for the Little League games
Where the players learn sportsmanship,
Where pitchers call nobody names
And the catchers give nobody lip.
Where the bench warmers never pout
And losers are taught not to grump,
And where, if a man is called out,
Only Mama yells: "Kill the ump!"

MOM'S NEW COIF-FUROR

As shy as a girl at a prom,
I awaited my dear ones' view:
The kids cried, 'What's for dinner, Mom?'
And my spouse exclaimed, "What's new?"

OKAY, PARENTS, LET'S HEAR IT!

Two, four, six, eight
Who do we appreciate?
Who do we admire, adore,
Even run the flag up for?
Who's the hero, who's the champ?
The man who runs the Boy Scout camp!

WINDOW WASHING

A little job done best by three;
One in, one out, one referee.

SALE WAIL

The dress that's elegant and queen-ish,
The one that's strictly steal-the-scene-ish,
The one that makes your friends turn green-ish
Is size nine if you're 14-ish.

BRIDE'S COOK BOOK

You'll find that half that many noodles
Makes oodles.

RUN! RUN!

In rain or snow or sleet or fog,
At 6 o'clock each morn I jog.
I don my sweatshirt with a smile,
And trot along my metered mile.
My heart is hale, my lungs are stout,
But, Lord, my feet are giving out!

HOMO SAPIENS AT PLAY

When single
He'll mingle,
But married we find
He hunches
In bunches
With those of his kind.

MIXED GREENS

My salad garden's green and sleek;
I planted all the yard
With lettuce, radishes and leek,
Plus peppers, parsley, chard.

And every single seed I threw
Came up without a hitch;
But omigosh, I wish I knew
Which was which.

UNHAPPY RETURNS

What thieves don't steal or moths corrupt,
Your form ten-forty gobbles up.

HEAVY HEART

A visit to the doctor sends
A tremor through me. Oh, my friends,
The instrument which makes me quail
Is not his scalpel: it's his scale.

ELEMENTARY VICTORY

The banquet fare was hearty,
The caps and gowns had dash.
The prom and post-prom party
Were definitely smash.
For days we've celebrated,
Our pride cannot be reckoned;
'Cause Junior's graduated
From first grade into second.

HOME GROAN TOMATOES

You set the little seedlings out,
And when the leaves begin to sprout
You build a little fence of string
And fertilize like anything.
You chase away the greedy birds
And whisper tender, loving words,
And then your produce reaches peak
While you are at the shore some week.

KING FOR A DAY

Your home, my darling, is your castle,
And I, your wife, your loving vassal.
Behold, milord, your little nippers
Have run to fetch your pipe and slippers.
Your paper waits without a wrinkle
Beside your plate, and in a twinkle
All your loyal band will shout, "Hooray!"
Noble sire, this is ALLOWANCE DAY.

VACATION COTTAGE REVISITED

Where the paper drapes are wrinkled,
And the plumbing's out of hand,
And everything is sprinkled
With a gritty film of sand.
Where the screens have broken nettings,
And the kitchen closet sticks,
And they feature four place settings
For a family of six.
Where the mini-shower curtain
Makes me mad as a wet hen,
Yes, and where I'm almost certain
That next year we'll come again.

ABSENTEE REPARTEE

The saddest words of tongue or pen
Are those you didn't think of then.

MORNING WARNING

My disposition, pet, is prize;
I'm not a bit standoff-y,
But speak to me only with thine eyes
Until I've had my coffee!

DIRTY TRICK

Junior is home from Kamp Katydid,
And out on the porch he is stowing
His suitcase stuffed to the very lid
And a duffel bag overflowing.
I opened them up and took a peek,
And now I am lost in this quand'ry:
How can a kid be gone for a week
And bring home a month's worth of laundry?

THOUGHTS FOR THANKSGIVING

All that turkey, mince and pumpkin
Turns your thin kin into plump kin!

KINGHTLY PERFORMANCE

A husband is a courtly chap
Whose manners are superb;
Who never fails to tip his cap
Or walk beside the curb;
Who rescues gloves from off the floor,
And positively dives
To strike a match or hold a door
For other fellows' wives.

END OF AUGUST

Summer is losing
Some of its wattage;
The pipes are oozing
Down at the cottage.
Golf greens are browning,
Baseball is pallid;
Nobody's downing
Potato salad.
Kids are despairing,
But all of the while,
Mothers are wearing
The ghost of a smile.

TIP FROM A SEASONED TRAVELER

There's no trick to touring
With kids in the car;
I find some alluring
New games and a bar
Of candy, some snappy—
Type comics and piles
Of gum keep them happy—
For all of five miles!

NOVEMBER SONG

Sigh for those blessings forever gone by;
Turkey and dressings and three kinds of pie;
The table groaning with fruitcake and tart,
And no one consulting a calorie chart.

SLUMBER PARTY

Would you think me a dreary
Old backward number,
If I ventured to query:
WHEN do they slumber?

HOW TO WOO A WIFE

Don't fluster me with flowers,
Don't prance me out to dinner;
Don't dance with me for hours—
Just say you think I'm thinner.

CHRISTMAS VACATION

Brings glad hollers
From the scholars.

Lights the features
Of their teachers.

And spells doom
For guess whom.

ORIGINAL DESIGN

A gown with such a label
Is a thing to shout about.
In fact if I were able
I'd wear it inside out.

MOTHER'S DAY PRESENT FROM THE KIDS

After you've taken them to the store
And roamed the aisles for an hour or more;
After you've dropped them a subtle hint,
("Mother likes almond better than mint.")
After you've loaned them the three cents' tax,
And wrapped the package, you can relax;
Nothing to do till the day arrives
But practice your shouts of glad SURPRISE.

FATHER CHOOSES A CHRISTMAS TREE

He measures them with plumb
 and line,
And reads the grower's labels.
He ponders spruce and fir and pine,
And silver ones for tables.
He asks the man how prices run,
And if the needles drop off,
And then he buys the biggest one,
Goes home—and lops the top off.

WHO'S WHO AT THE SCHOOL PAGEANT

Some parents groan and grip their chairs
And scan the stage with anxious stares;
Others watch with carefree hearts—
Guess whose kids have speaking parts?

SEASON'S GRATING

Hail the office Christmas party,
Where the meekest clerk grows hearty;
Where the shyest secretary
Waxeth bold and maketh merry;
Where VIPs say, "Call me Joe!"
Beneath the plastic mistletoe;
Where spirits flow and laughter's rife,
And anything goes—except a wife.

RESOLVED

Now with another year at hand,
These resolutions I have planned;
    Start diet, give up sweets and bread.
    Turn off tv and read instead.
    Prepare a budget, make it stick.
    Explore the new arithmetic.
    Walk the dog when it is raining.
    Pay the bills without complaining.
You like them, dear? I'm glad you do.
It just so happens they're for you.

Made in the USA
Charleston, SC
14 December 2010